It is written...

Kamila Poonisamy

Presentation by *BookLeaf Publishing*

Web: www.bookleafpub.com

E-mail: info@bookleafpub.com

ISBN : 9789394788527

First edition 2022

For my family and loved ones.

For every person that has entered my life and
left a piece of treasure in my heart.

An Emerald Paradise.

A beautiful jewel
In the enormous, empty sea
Home, you were for me.

My proud place of birth
How you glisten in my heart
What a piece of art.

The secrets you hold
Legendary stories told
I wish I knew you.

One joyous day, I will
For now, glory to thee
O Sweet Motherland.

Unexpected Friendship

What an unexpected surprise.
Why do you ask?
The gift you give cannot be forgotten.
You love, support, mentor and nurture.
Unconditionally.

What an unexpected blessing.
Why do you ask?
Life changes when you are in it.
Your kindness, pureness, warmth and
compassion
is so unique to this world.

What an unexpected gift.
Why do you ask?
You listen, care, advise, and empower
every day, every night unconditionally.

An unexpected friendship no longer,
A blessing, honour, and privilege to call you
my friend, my family, my mentor.

Five Little Fingers

Five little fingers longed to be held.
My tears filled the oceans between us.
You heard my cries yet no one came running.
You were nowhere to be seen.

Five little fingers covered my big brown eyes.
You became the monster day and night.
As the sun sets, the tears flow
with your words running through my head.

Five little fingers no longer long for you.
The words you give no longer hold value.
You are everywhere to be seen but
no longer needed. Words can hurt.
These five little fingers are little no more.

O Sweet Souls

I once held you in my arms,
just as I was once held by you.
Sweet souls you are now free
from the chains of humanity.
These branches that connected us,
are damaged but not broken.
I miss you every time the sun rises
and the moon glows.
You may not be here with me
but you are at peace.
I see your smile every day,
Your laughter can be heard every night.
Sleep now sweet souls
for now you are divine memories.

Everyone needs to...

Raise your children to
Embrace their identity,
Serenade their desires.
Patience can help but
Empathy is free
Compassion is needed
To teach respect for one and another.

A Mother's Blessing

This tempest was unknown.
Her eyes gazing at the victims
Her mouth devouring everything in her way.
As her feet touch the ground,
The Earth trembled beneath it.

As quickly as she approached,
She had disappeared.
The force of a mother could not be matched.
Tempers flared which only her child could
pacify.

There was a relief in feeling the storm's
approach.
The rain pelting against my skin. My hair
blowing in the wind.
What a blessing!
With the Sun blazing brightly,
Mother is smiling at me.

A Woman's role

I am a daughter.
You raised me to think, feel, speak.
Be independent.

I am a sister.
I stand strong on my two feet.
Be kind, calm, caring.

I am a great friend.
If you need me, I am here.
No doubt in my mind.

I am a woman.
Empower and inspire.
No labels needed.

Deep Breaths

Take a deep breath.
Count one, two, three.
As your mind wanders,
Look for a tree.

Take a deep breath.
Count four, five, six.
Listen out for those
Satisfying little tweets

Take a deep breath.
Count one, two, three.
As you take a step,
Smell that fresh cut grass.

Take a deep breath.
Count four, five, six.
Turn that corner,
Feel the wind caress your skin.

Take a deep breath.
Count one, two, three.
Take a seat,
For deep breaths take up far more space
Than silence.

Forgiven But Not Forgotten

Your actions were once so kind
Yet your words broke my soul.
You said we were a puzzle
Yet these pieces could not fit.
You said I could aim for the sky
Yet you dictated what I wanted.
You said to be yourself
Yet you did not see it.
You said do not fear
Yet you became the thing I did.
You brought me gifts
Yet you made me pay with tears.
You took me on adventures
Yet our destination was unknown,
I can forgive
But I am yet to forget.

Dawn

I was never an early riser
Until I had a reason to be.
The Sun calls me everyday
My bed holds me before I'm ready.

I never was an early riser.
My dreams flourished
Waiting to be free.
The warmth that cuddles me.
Why is it so hard to leave?

I never was an early riser
Until it was clear to me
Life's too short to waste away
What potentially awaits for me?

I never was an early riser
I can't wait to start my day
5 am, the golden hour
When will I have this time ever again?

Pursuing Happiness

Happy
A strange concept
A mystery for us
Can it be achieved today?
One day.

Just Act Natural

Small talk needed!
What's the weather like today?
How was your weekend?
Did you have a good day?
Just act natural.

Speak properly!
Articulate your ideas.
Elevate your vocabulary.
Don't drop those 't's or 'g's
Just fit in.

Dress smart
Put on make up
Straighten your hair
Wear those heels
Just look good.

Be proud!
Break those stereotypes
Go beyond expectations
Just be you.

Live, Love, Laugh

Live life to the fullest.
Mistakes can be made
But lessons need to be learnt.
It's ok to cry,
Try not to hurt.
Life can be hard but
In the end, we only regret the chances we did not
take.

Love deeply to the greatest.
Acquaintances exist
Whilst peers can resist.
Friendships are needed but
Relationships are a bonus.
Love can be devastating, however,
In the end, we only regret the chances we did not
take.

Laugh the hardest.
For life is too short
For us to take it for granted.
Make those special memories,
For in the end, we only regret the chances we
did not take.

Jelly and Chai

The future was uncertain
And companionship was a notion of doubt
But love was the least that filled my heart
As I wished to share with all who cared.

Then came the University days
Where we all met,
and built a bond never to regret.
You became a part of my family and company,
Giving me fulfillment and encouragement.

Days were full of studying English and French.
As we blended it with unforgettable memories
Of bowling in a trench. Shopping like a bunch of
hoarders.
Coupled with laughter and fast spoken moments
in places both old and new.
What adventures we had, whilst skipping the
queues.

Friendship sure took meaning from you both
As you have been my safety net during my highs
and lows
Giving me love in all our craziness and laughter
We share an unbreakable bond like daughters of
the same mother. ★

Have courage to speak the truth!

Caution, take a step back.
Open those eyes of yours!
Under that tough skin, you feel the pain within.
Rage forever burns inside, until you
Acclimate. Respect.
Gauge those in sheep's clothing. Friends or
Enemies? Who knows?

A Father's Teaching

Grab a rod and reel.
What a deal!
Flick your wrist,
and make a wish.

Grab your pens and pencils.
Paint your stencils.
What a work of art,
All from the heart.

Grab a bat and ball,
A game for all.
Aim for the sky,
Don't be shy.

Grab a Gi and a belt,
Yell until your heart melts.
Kekomi, Mae Geri, Mawashi Geri
Zodan, Chudan, Gedan Barai.

Let your mind flourish,
And let there be no anguish.
Creativity run free,
For you need more than a degree.

Where There's A Will, There's A Way.

Which way to go?
What a great show.
Which advice to seek?
Nothing too meek.

Plan, Plot, Preserve.
Don't hit that nerve.
Keep your head on straight,
And your mind great.
The goal is fate.

So many obstacles,
Which one to tackle?
Listen to the voice within.
For it is the origin.

Peace, Present, Perspective.
This is what we need.
Don't get lead astray,
For where there's a will, there's a way.

Never Give Up

Not in this life, will
Everyone resist. The
Very vibrant, thriving
Essence of life,
Results in trials and tribulations.

God gave us hope, to live
In peace, harmony and
Virtue. Yet we choose to
Evaluate our servitude.

Uprise against the temptations. As it is for the
People, that great barriers were created.

The Destructive Seven

Power, Status, Money.
Does that make you feel better?
7.9 billion people in this world
Yet, in the end you are alone.

Pleasure, Attraction, Passion.
Does that make you feel good?
A primal urge. What an excuse!
In the end, NO means NO.

Winner, Possession, Rights
Do you feel satisfied?
The latest trends and technology.
In the end, it will never be enough.

Desire, Resentment, Grudges
Do you feel admired?
The perfect body, perfect life, perfect job.
In the end, what is perfection? Just be you.

Pain, Rage, Fury
Does this give you strength?
Projecting fear for your own gain,
Yet in the end, wisdom will conquer all.

Indulgence, Comfort, Binge.
Do you live in this luxury?
689 million people living in poverty
Yet, in the end, you do not care.

Boredom, Despair, Ungrateful.
You are entitled, right?
Education, Food, Water, Clothes, Relationships.
Yet, in the end you do not work for it.

The Resident.

The glorious blue room.
A place for a warrior, protector, defender.
What great fun you are.
Full of adventure, an accomplice.
A place to grow, to learn, to play.

The magnificent purple room.
For an intellect, counsellor, mentor.
What great comfort you are.
A partner in crime, full of wisdom.
A place to cry, to reflect, to nurture.

The many adventures we had.
Day after day, night after night.
The many memories we will make.
What such pride I have to be a resident in both
rooms.

It is Written...

It has been an interesting journey,
Full of obstacles and achievements.
But each one is a lesson learnt.
How grateful I am for all I go through,
For each event is unique to me.
No one else can say,
They have gone through the same.
As this is what makes me. My identity.
The glow slowly grows each day.
No one can take that away.
What is left to experience,
A great story untold.
It is already written,
Ready to be explored.